The Checklist Workshop

How to make
great checklists – for
more quality, efficiency
and clarity

Alexander Nerá

Bibliografische Information der Deutschen Nationalbibliothek:
Die Deutsche Nationalbibliothek verzeichnet diese Publikation in der
Deutschen Nationalbibliografie; detaillierte bibliografische Daten sind im
Internet über http://dnb.dnb.de abrufbar.

Umschlagbild / Cover Picture:
Pixabay

Herstellung und Verlag / Published by:
BoD – Books on Demand, Norderstedt

ISBN: 978-3753435800

Contents

Introduction   5

    The New Hires   5

    A Storage Rack   6

    The Missing Swimsuit   7

To the Sceptical Reader   9

    'I don't know what to put on a checklist.'   9

    'It's too much work.'   10

    'Everyone already knows how to do that.' 10

What do We Mean by Checklist?   12

A First Approach   16

Designing the Checklist   21

    Versions of Checklists   22

    Title   23

    Instances of Checklists   24

    One Action per Step   25

    Conditional Steps   26

    Numbering the Tasks   27

Date Completed or Tick   27

Actionable Now or Later   28

Several Predecessors   30

Iterative Actions   31

Reference Material   33

Responsible Parties   33

Results   34

Time and Effort   34

Combinations   34

Generating Content   37

Exploration   37

Document Review   39

Simulation   40

Working Backwards   43

Summary   46

Case Study: Susan's Checklist   48

Designing the Checklist   48

Gathering Content   49

The Final Result   54

Conclusion   56

Index   58

Introduction

The New Hires

Susan sat down at her desk in the personnel department. It was the first day of the month, her favourite day. Susan was the company's recruiting expert. After months of discussing staff requirements with the department heads, posting job advertisements, interviews with applicants and preparing the employment contracts and other paperwork, today was the day when she could finally welcome her new colleagues.

Susan loved working with people, so she considered any kind of administrative task a necessary evil, but after almost three years with the company she thought she knew how to handle the boring stuff. As proof, welcome packages and access cards lay in front of hear, ready to be handed over.

At eight minutes to nine the front desk rang and announced the arrival of the new hires. Susan would go to pick them up immediately, but first she opened a drawer to take out the envelopes that contained the computer login details. Rather than e-mailing this information to her, the head of IT insisted that it be sent by internal mail. Susan found it funny that access to the company's digital world come by paper only. She reached for the envelopes – they were not there! That was impossible!

Thinking hard for a moment, Susan realized that she had no recollection of receiving the envelopes. They usually arrived a couple of days in advance. It took IT three days to send them after she had requested the login details. She always did that by phone to make sure that the colleague at IT who was handling the matter would pick the right employee from the database. And she had given them a call about a week ago – oh, she froze – that was when the database was down and the kind IT specialist had asked her to call again an hour later.

Which she had forgotten to do.

A Storage Rack

Jim liked woodworking. It was his favourite hobby, and he had become quite good at it over the years. He had built tables and wooden boxes with hidden compartments. His masterpiece was a bookcase that had a moving section which could be opened to reveal more storage space behind the book shelves.

The current project was less exciting. It was a plain storage rack for his garage. The construction was simple and symmetrical: three vertical boards would carry the horizontal shelves. Jim thought the middle board would give it enough stability, so he could just glue everything together.

All pieces were sanded already. He drilled the holes for the dowels. Jim was bored and wanted to be done with it. As the construction was no challenge, he decided he would just put glue on all the parts and clamp everything in one go. He would need to be quick, but he had assembled more complicated pieces before.

He used a brush for the glue. Working quickly, he could not avoid smudges but would worry about them later. He put one vertical board flat on the floor and put the dowels and shelf boards into the right places. Now he had to fit the middle board on top of the seven shelf boards. The dowels didn't go into the holes right away; at least one of the pieces always sat askew.

Damn, this was taking too much time. He became worried about the glue settling. Finally, the middle board was in place. One half done!

Next came the shelve boards for the other side of the rack. They were waiting on his joiner's bench and had to go on top of the middle board. When he reached for them, he noticed there were only six pieces. Where was the seventh? He had done fourteen shelf boards in total, had he not?

Without the seventh piece, he could not clamp the second half. He had to clamp the half that was already assembled before the glue dried, though! But he needed to get the glue off the loose pieces if he wanted to be able to use them later!

Why had he not counted all the pieces before putting glue on everything?

The Missing Swimsuit

Robert and Jill had checked into a luxury resort in Florida. It was the first time they had gone on holiday in over a year. Robert ran his own consultancy firm that advised logistic companies on complex projects. He was a project manager by heart and had checklists and assessment tables for everything – both at home and in the office. The resort they were in was not a random pick, of course, but number one on Robert's Recreation Destinations List.

Jill did not mind his checklist obsession most of the time or rather ignored it whenever possible. Regarding their current journey, however, she had found it necessary to intervene: when she had noticed that several south-east Asian islands were leading the destination list, she had pointed out to Robert that the Political Stability criterion might be under-weighed. The revised ranking of the destinations was more to her liking.

Robert was already in his swim trunks. 'What about a dive in the pool?' he asked.

'I must have left my swimming togs at home,' Jill answered. 'I'll have to do some shopping first.'

'You didn't bring a bathing suit?' Robert was incredulous. 'It's on the packing list!'

'Are you sure? Well, maybe I didn't use the right version.'

Jill called the front desk to order a taxi.

'I am sure it is on *every* list because there may always be an indoor pool,' insisted Robert while he switched on his notebook to review the checklists.

'Never mind,' Jill answered unperturbed. 'I am sure they do sell swimwear in Florida.' And why would she bring old bathing suits when she could buy new ones here? But she didn't say that out loud.

*

Robert and Jill will be fine. This book is for the Jims and Susans among us – people who are enthusiastic about their jobs but desire some help with the mundane and mechanical tasks.

Checklists come in many forms. I have seen scribbles on sticky notes, plain text files, and sophisticated (or not so sophisticated) spread sheets. The types of checklists are as varied as the complaints people have made about them: incomplete, with items in the wrong order, outdated, redundant, unclear, misleading, ugly, …

If you need checklists but sometimes struggle with them, join the Checklist Workshop. This book contains many concepts and techniques for creating checklists. It is meant to give you a wide range of options to choose from and combine according to your situation.

The following chapters include many examples – good and bad, some only to illustrate the use of a layout element. Examples that are examined in some depth are marked with ⚒.

To the Sceptical Reader

My assumption about you is that you think there is a benefit in using checklists. When you look for ways to create helpful checklists and ideas to design and adjust them according to your needs, there are a lot of concepts and tools in this book for you.

I am sure there are people who dislike checklists or think that, in their particular situation, checklists are unnecessary. I will not argue with the former and agree that the latter may be the case. I would like, however, to invite those readers to review with me three common arguments against checklists. If afterwards you are still convinced that checklists are not for you – that's fine. But perhaps you can understand the checklist aficionados a little bit better.

'I don't know what to put on a checklist.'

If you have the slightest suspicion that checklists may be helpful to you in your area of expertise, I am convinced you also have the necessary know-how regarding the contents. Otherwise, the thought would not have come up. As for the preparation, structure and form of checklists, this book will help you and show you principles you can apply.

Using a checklist in one situation doesn't mean that you will never again do anything without ticking off a task. But the knowledge of the tools described this book can help you to decide if making a checklist is useful in a particular situation.

'It's too much work.'

Granted – making a checklist means additional work beforehand. The question is if the payoff is worth the effort in the long run.

How much time will you save if you don't have to think about the tasks or their order and can focus on one single task after another?

How much will you benefit from the knowledge that you have done everything you planned to do and not forgotten anything?

How much easier will it be to continue working on something you had to postpone if you can see at a glance where you stopped earlier?

'Everyone already knows how to do that.'

The purpose of a checklist is not to teach you anything, as opposed to a manual. Pilots, for example, are well-known for using checklists before and while flying a plane to the next destination. Considering this use of checklists, I am adamant that checklists are not teaching material. Here are some examples for what a checklist can be:

· a reminder to do something,

· documentation that you have done something[1],

· a means to help you get an overview about a line of actions, so you can reconsider when to do them, how much time they might take or if you should delegate anything.

Checklists tell you *that* things should be done – not how.

---

[1] By checking off the tasks or noting the date when you have completed one (see page 27).

If you are not convinced yet, I would like to propose the following compromise: people don't need checklists for everything. Also, a useful checklist can mean different things to different persons. Then again, there are undertakings for which a checklist is unsuitable or not powerful enough.

The next chapter discusses the kind of checklists this book is about.

What do We Mean by Checklist?

I have used the term 'checklist' rather casually in the previous chapters. Before we move on to making checklists, we should agree on what we mean by the word.

On the next pages, I would like to explain what I consider a checklist for the purpose of this book and what the intention of this kind of checklists is.

Taking the word literally, a checklist can be any list of items (usually words or expressions) that you can check off, cross out, or simply marvel at. You can call any to-do list, shopping list, or packing list a *checklist.*

🛠 Imagine office worker Alice coming back from her lunch break. She could be making a to-do list ad hoc, so she won't forget what she wants to do before leaving the office for the day. It could look like this:

Call back Steve
Finish travel expense report
Print sales agreement for review
Stock up on paper clips
E-mail agenda of next week's meeting to assistant

I encourage you to keep making this kind of lists, but please note that the list is specific to that particular day. The number of items on the list is so small that their order doesn't really matter. Most items are not related to or dependent on others on the list. After Alice has done the tasks, the list will not be of much help for the next day.

For the checklists we discuss in this book, rather the opposite is true:

- I assume that you will have the need to refer to them on a recurring basis.

- The items of a checklist are dependent on each other or, at least, are related to a common overall topic.

- Working through them will lead to a specific outcome.

- Deleting any action item can impact the overall result.

Checklists like these are used by pilots before take-off or for preparing a monthly company newsletter to the staff.

On the other hand, there are documents that are beyond the scope of checklists and, thus, beyond the scope of this book. This would typically include manuals, project plans and the documentation of business processes:

- **Manuals:** A manual is not a checklist because a checklist does not teach you how to do things. A manual does. If you don't know how to use a certain software, a look into the manual should be helpful. Most of us would not read the whole manual but use it as a reference when needed and only read the section that explains the desired function. Even if a manual describes the steps to reach a certain result, it will usually contain explanations. Checklist are focused on the steps only[2].

---

[2] It is quite common, however, to mention reference material on checklists (see page 33).

- **Project Plans:** A project plan is usually much longer than a checklist. Also, projects are unique one-of-a-kind endeavours, so they tend to be less standardized than checklists. Another difference is that the number of people working on the same project plan will be larger than that of persons using a common checklist.

- **Business Processes:** A business process is highly standardized and can involve few or many people. Both checklists and business processes can stretch over weeks and month. A business process may have a larger scope than a checklist, but that's not always the case. The documentation of many a business process is based on checklists that were updated and used by individual employees for years. And that is not the worst basis you could imagine. Business processes within one company are often documented in a specified format.

All these types of lists and documentation have things in common, and the boundaries are often blurred. Just as a well-designed checklist may become part of a business process, a person on a project team might take a list of actions out of the project plan and treat it as a personal checklist before reporting back to the project manager.

The following diagram compares the checklists covered in this book to other (non-reference) documents in terms of complexity and standardisation:

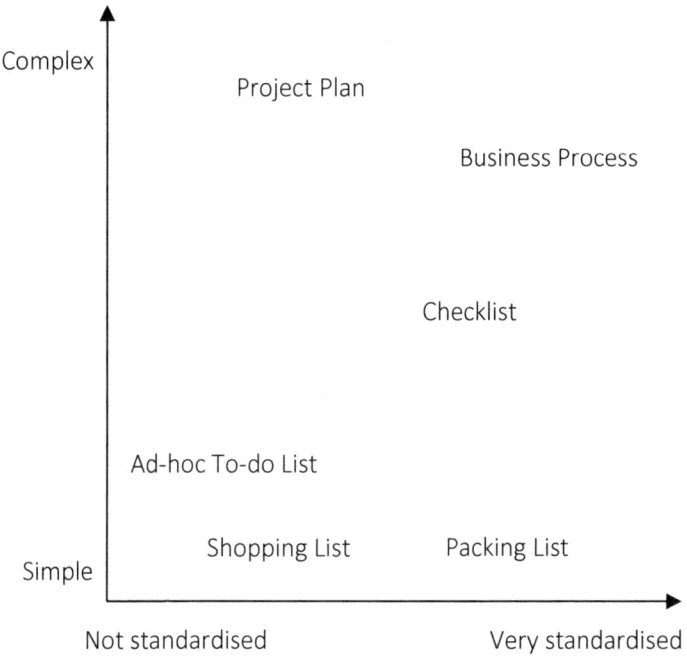

When you are willing to go forward on this basis, why don't we begin by taking apart a recipe for cooking pasta?

A First Approach

In order to determine some basic criteria for what makes a good checklist, let's look at a simple example – we are going to analyse the instructions for cooking pasta.

'Wait a moment!' you might think. 'I know how to cook pasta, and I don't really care how the instructions are written.'

I picked this example exactly for that reason. Pretending that cooking pasta is a very special task, we will ask which instructions inexperience cooks might struggle with.

⚒ Recipes about cooking pasta can be easily found on the internet. I compiled the following text from various fragments, so it can serve as a case study:

> Step 1
> To cook the pasta, pour approximately 1 litre of water per 100 g of dry pasta into a large saucepan and bring it to a boil. Stir in 1 teaspoon of salt per litre of water, then add the pasta. For a main course you need 100–125 g of dry pasta per person.
>
> Step 2
> Cook the pasta in boiling water. Stir it again and again so that the noodles do not stick to each other. Dry noodles usually cook for about 8–10 minutes.

Step 3
Shortly before the end of the specified cooking time, test
to see whether the pasta is done. Depending on the
desired consistency – firm to the bite or soft – continue
cooking the pasta. After the pasta is cooked, drain the
pasta in a sieve.

Let's look at the instructions step-by-step and see whether they are
explicit and complete:

Step 1

☺ I recommend numbering the steps. It allows making references
to a specific action, either when speaking with someone about the
checklist or when an action depends on an earlier one. It is no
irrevocable rule, though. We will come back to the topic on page 27.

To cook the pasta, …

☹ Always make clear what your checklist is about in a description
or title at the top. Mentioning the purpose of the entire list as part
of a step increases the text without adding value.

… pour approximately 1 litre of water per 100 g of dry
pasta into a large saucepan and bring it to a boil. Stir in 1
teaspoon of salt per litre of water, then add the pasta.

☹ There are several actions in this step. This should be avoided in
a well-structured checklist because you would struggle to check off
a part of the instructions when the rest is not done yet.

As you have to wait for the water to start boiling, the
completion of this step is not entirely in your control. Hence, you
can neither consider this action complete nor continue with your
work. It's better to split this into two actions.

Whether the addition of salt and pasta should be one or two tasks, is up to your preference and experience.

> For a main course you need 100–125 g of dry pasta per person.

☹ The purpose of a checklist is not to teach its user anything. On the other hand, it might be convenient to include relevant information material in the checklist. The additional information here is how much pasta you need per person (see section 'Reference Material' on page 33 about how to distinguish tasks from background information). The big problem, however, is that this information comes too late! It turns out that the amount of water depends on the amount of pasta which depends on the amount per person. The last piece of information is given only *after* you have heated the water and added the pasta. The items on a checklist should be ordered so that you can work through them consecutively.

> Step 2
> Cook the pasta in boiling water. Stir it again and again so that the noodles do not stick to each other. Dry noodles usually cook for about 8–10 minutes.

☺ This direction is clearly structured. Note that it describes things going on in parallel (cooking pasta, pasta being stirred), so this action cannot be split in two. It also gives you information about the usual cooking time.

> Step 3
> Shortly before the end of the specified cooking time, test to see whether the pasta is done. Depending on the desired consistency – firm to the bite or soft – continue

cooking the pasta. After the pasta is cooked, drain the
pasta in a sieve.

☹ It turns out that there is a fatal problem with 'step 2' and 'step 3':
after 10 minutes of cooking, as the previous instruction suggests,
you move on to 'step 3' – and find the pasta is overcooked.

A task in a checklist should never tell you what you should have
done *before* you completed a previous step.

Stop here for a moment, take a pen and try to transform these
instructions into a foolproof checklist.

*

This is my proposal for a revised checklist that avoids the problems
pointed out above:

Checklist: Cooking Pasta

1	Procure the required amount of pasta. *Note: For a main course you need 100–125 g of dry pasta per person.*
2	Pour approximately 1 litre of water per 100 g of dry pasta into a large saucepan.
3	Bring the water to a boil.
4	Stir in 1 teaspoon of salt per litre of water.
5	Add the pasta.
6	Cook the pasta in boiling water for approximately 7 minutes. Stir it again and again so that the noodles do not stick to each other. *Note: Dry noodles usually cook for about 8–10 minutes.*
7	Test to see whether the pasta is done. Depending on the desired consistency – firm to the bite or soft – continue cooking the pasta.
8	Drain the pasta in a sieve.

You will find that all tasks were included in the original version –
except step 1. Why did I add a further task? As we noted before,
the number of persons defines the required amount of pasta and

indirectly the required amount of water. Accordingly, the amount of pasta has to be determined before we can start cooking. Since we already know the amount, it is convenient to prepare the required amount of pasta as well.

In general, a checklist should make clear what needs to be done when, so you can work through the steps one by one. That's what checklists are about after all.

You will notice that the pasta will not be ready at the end of task 6. That is intentional. The cooking will likely have to be continued in task 7, but only after you have tried the pasta.

In the next chapter, we will compile our toolbox of elements for creating a customized checklist layout.

Designing the Checklist

In this chapter, we will cover concepts and structural elements that make your checklists clearer, more convenient to use, and easier to update. This is pretty formal stuff, but the more support you get from the layout of your checklist, the more you can focus on the actual tasks.

A checklist should help you working through the tasks. The handling of a checklist should not cause additional effort.

How much time and consideration you spend on the structure and the design depends on the complexity of the tasks, on how often you are going to use the checklist, and on your personal preferences.

'Should we not concern ourselves with the contents of a checklist before we decide on the design?' you might ask.

My recommendation is that you begin with the design. When you start putting together a checklist, you will have at least a general idea and maybe even old notes or an old version of a checklist. That gives you a sufficient basis for making basic design decisions. As you are likely to prepare your checklist with some kind of software, you will be able to make adjustments later.

If you begin with adding tasks to a list, you make implicit decisions about the structure. If it turns out that a different approach would be better, it is my experience that people are often too lazy[3] to change it later.

---

[3] I meant to say 'busy', of course.

✗ Bob and his team want to create a list that keeps track of documents to be sent from one department to another. One of the action items could be:

Sales report by Sales Manager to be sent to Controlling

After they have gathered a dozen similar items, someone might suggest that separate columns for sender and receiver would be much clearer. Perhaps like this:

Document	Sender	Receiver
Sales Report	Sales Manager	Controlling

Let's assume that everyone agrees that this format is a good idea. If this would happen in your team and you can be sure that everyone will agree to work through all the steps again and split them into document, sender, and receiver – fine. If you doubt that all team members will gladly revisit every task to make it fit the new columns, spend a few minutes thinking about the layout first.

Versions of Checklists

It is advisable to put a date or a version number on your checklist whenever you are using a checklist more than once or if it is going to develop over time. That is more likely than one might think when 'just taking down some steps I have to do'. If you are not sure that the list you are making is only an ad-hoc to-do list (see page 12), consider the following questions:

· Do you expect to add steps, to add references or that references will change?

- Are you going to use the list as a template for other lists (for example, you intend to use your general packing list as a basis for packing lists for business trips, weekend trips, etc.)?

- Will you share your checklist with others who may send back comments or even an updated version?

- Is it possible that other people will update the template of your checklist?[4]

If any of the above apply, I strongly recommend adding a version or a date[5]. The effort of doing so is negligible when you compare it with the time saved if you do *not* need to match two lists line by line in order to find out who worked with which version.

Title

It might seem trivial, but as soon as you have more than one checklist – and if you are reading this book, you are a suspect – you should put on top of the list what it is about. You will be able to distinguish the steps for planning a business trip from those of handling a customer complaint, of course, but remember that the

---

[4] Other people updating your tools is always a double-edged sword. On the one hand, their contribution is likely to be more specific than, e.g., 'we should add more details in the middle section when all the documents are prepared'. On the other hand, they might not adhere to the layout principles you have selected after careful consideration.

[5] It's generally a good idea to date any notes you make during meetings or phone calls. Here is a quick calculation: let's assume that you need three seconds to add a date to your handwritten notes. If it sometimes becomes relevant to know when you took the notes and if we assume that it will take you two minutes to find the respective entry in your diary, you can put 40 futile dates on meeting notes before you will have wasted time overall.

checklist is there to help you and not make you work out what it should tell you loud and clear.

This is what you should *not* use as title for your checklist:

Checklist

But rather:

Checklist: Customer Complaints

Instances of Checklists

Expanding the principle of the previous section, I recommend providing for information above your checklists that lets you distinguish different instances. This is relevant when you are going to use more than one checklist of the same type in parallel – for example, if you are planning several events at the same time. It's a good idea to apply this even to trivial sets of tasks – to avoid mistaking one for the other

🛠 Alice has organized two events that take place at the same time. Imaging the embarrassment if the speaker for one event were not there because Alice forgot to confirm the date – and the speaker at the event in the other room is annoyed because she has asked him repeatedly if he is available that day. Just make a little space under the title where you can jot down what event the list is used for:

Checklist: Event Planning

Event: *Annual Staff Meeting on 14 June*

One Action per Step

I have advocated before that each entry or step of your checklist should contain a single action. What a single action is, depends on the user of the checklist and the familiarity with the task. When it was common to send letters by post, the following entry may have sufficed:

Action
Prepare envelope

As mailing letters is not done so often anymore, more detailed content[6] may be useful:

Action
Write address on envelope
Put stamp in upper right corner
Seal envelope

How much detail your list should include is a content issue (more on content on page 37 ff).

The point here is that I advise thinking twice before making a list within a list. Take the example above: why not put the three steps of the second table as sub-entries under 'prepare envelope'?

In my experience, the sub-list is likely to become outdated because it will always be a self-contained element and people are hesitant to make changes to what is tried and tested. Also, when a new task needs to be added, it may not really fit into the context of the sub-list. It is then put in before or after, even if it would fit best between the tasks of the sub-list.

---

[6] Remember this section is about the structure of checklists. We will come back to the content of this example in the section 'Simulation' on page 40.

Conditional Steps

There may be tasks in your checklist that are relevant or can be done only after certain conditions are met. I recommend separating those conditions from the task, i.e., if you ignore the condition, the rest of the entry should read like a task.

The following should be avoided:

> Also, the Compliance department needs to be contacted when we order from a new supplier in case they have requirements which the supplier does not clearly meet.

Instead:

Action
If new supplier: Involve Compliance

If you have a lot of conditional actions, it might be advisable to make the distinction even clearer, e.g., by bold type:

Action
If new supplier: Involve Compliance

'Wait a moment!' you might object. 'When there is a condition and it does apply, there may be not only one, but a series of actions I have to do. I don't want to put the condition before every single task. But you said I should not put a list within a single entry. How are you going to resolve that?'

That's a valid point, and I maintain that a list within a list should be avoided when the items on the sub-list are not clearly subordinated to the item on the main list. Bear with me for now, or – if you can't – have a peek at my solution on page 29.

Numbering the Tasks

In general, numbering tasks is a matter of personal taste. Some people don't see much benefit in putting a number in front of each step because they are listed one after another anyway. Why bother? There is also the disadvantage that you have to re-number everything when you add or delete a task.

Other people cannot imagine a list of discrete steps without putting a number in front of each. Discussions about this question have become more heated than one would expect, so I will tread carefully: if it doesn't matter, do as you like.

There are a few cases, however, when numbering can be useful. Here are two examples:

· When you discuss the checklist or the status of the checklist with someone, it is easier to refer to 'step 17' rather than 'the one about calling the agency, fifth from below'.

· Numbers are useful when you want to make references within the checklist:

#	Action
10	If event is online: Skip steps 11 – 13
11	Inform front desk about name of guests
12	...
13	...
14	...

Date Completed or Tick

When hearing 'checklist', most people imagine a list of tasks and a column with check marks (ticks). If all actions are completed within a short period of time or if it doesn't matter when they were done, check marks will do. But what if it is important when an action was done – or when it *could* be convenient to know?

Imagine you need to request a piece of information from a business partner. It says so on your checklist, and you send an e-mail asking for that information. But you get no response. More often than not, when you remind them, they want to know when you asked for the information. If you have an e-mail, you can look up the date. If you requested it by phone, there is no record. Either way – wouldn't it be convenient if you could just take a look at your checklist and tell them when you requested the information?

Action	Done
Request new sales figures from controlling	7 Mar

Actionable Now or Later

There may be actions you have to postpone for the moment, e.g., because they are to be done only after a certain date. On a quiet afternoon in August, for example, you will not take the Christmas decoration out of the basement.

Often, people like to put general information on checklists when certain tasks should be done. Go ahead and include the general rule on the list, but *also* add a field where you can put the date for the specific instance. All actions dependent on that date can be listed after that. Use the symbol ↳ to indicate that an action depends on an entry above.

In the following example, the date '10 April' has been derived from the general rule ('two weeks'):

Due	Action	Done
10 Apr	Do two weeks before new employee starts	
↳	...	
↳	...	

The same structure can be applied when something needs to happen before you can tackle certain tasks. In that case, put the condition on your list and add a field (it's the box in the example below) you can tick when the condition has been fulfilled. Ticking that field 'activates' the dependent tasks:

Due	Action	Done
☐	Do when applicant has accepted job offer	
↳	...	
↳	...	

As promised on page 26, we have now the tool to avoid a sub-list when a series of tasks depends on a condition. And neither do we need to repeat the condition before each action:

Due	Action	Done
☐	New Supplier	
↳	Involve Compliance	
↳	Check credit rating	
↳	...	

One remark about numbering when using separate lines for conditions: as a matter of personal preference, I tend not to assign a number to those lines since they usually do not constitute an action. In the table above, the lines marked with ↳ would be numbered, but the one with ☐ would not. This is just a way to distinguish conditions from actions, but does not have any further consequence.

What should we do with unconditional tasks that do not depend on anything? You can simply put nothing, knowing that an empty field means the task can be done when you have the time to do it.

It may be difficult to distinguish between the unconditional tasks and those where the due date has not been filled in or that have not been 'activated' yet. Rather than leaving it empty, I recommend putting 'ASAP' into the Due column or any symbol that's meaningful to you.

I have used ★ in the following example:

Due	Action	Done
★	Water office plant	
★	Check e-mails	

Several Predecessors

Some tasks may become due or actionable only several previous tasks have been completed. If that is the case, you can put the numbers of the preceding tasks into the Due column before the dependent task (e.g., in a lighter colour).

In the following example, the maker of the checklist plans an event. He or she has invited a speaker and wants to send *one* confirmation with all pieces of information to the speaker. Therefore, tasks 5, 6, and 9 have to be completed before the confirmation can be sent (task 15):

#	Due	Action	Done
5	★	Book room	
6	★	Have agenda approved by supervisor	
...			
9	★	Minimum number of registrations achieved	
...			
15	5 6 9	Send confirmation to speaker	

When you are still expanding your checklist a lot and are concerned that you might forget updating the reference numbers, you can repeat the prerequisites:

#	Due	Action	Done
15	5	**If room booked:**	
	6	**If agenda approved:**	
	9	**If minimum number of participants achieved:**	
	✍	Send confirmation to speaker	

Iterative Actions

There are cases when completing an action is not one step but several – but each is closely tied to the other.

✘ Bob runs a project office and it's his task to maintain the project documentation. Since no member of the project team ever sends him anything without being reminded, he has to go through the same steps for every document:

> Ask for the document
> Make sure document is received
> Check if document is signed and includes appendixes
> File document

Instead of repeating these four tasks on his checklist for every document, Bob converts them into four columns:

Document	Requested	Received	Reviewed	Filed
Project Proposal				
...				
...				

If you don't like the horizontal entries per document because you prefer working through a checklist from top to bottom, you can use the following structure:

Document	Action	Date
Project Proposal	Requested	
	Received	
	Reviewed	
	Filed	
...	Requested	
	Received	
	Reviewed	
	Filed	

The tasks refer to a specific document, so the 4-item sub-lists are not likely to cause problems – even though I generally advise against lists within lists.

This form has another benefit: if certain steps are not required for some documents, you can simply leave them out. When you use columns for each action, you are stuck with the structure. You could leave fields empty if you don't need them. But the empty fields will stand out, and you will always be drawn to check why they are empty.

Crossing them out is an option. If you know which fields you don't need when preparing the checklist, you can do that already in the template of the checklist.

🛠 Let's consider Bob and the project office again. If he has sent the agenda of a meeting to the project team, he doesn't have to ask for the document before he can file it.

Document	Requested	Received	Reviewed	Filed
Agenda	X	X	X	
Project Proposal				

Reference Material

While a checklist should not become a manual, it is often convenient to include background information, guidelines or reference material. In these cases, the action should be clearly distinguished from the additional information, for example:

Action	Done
Send invitation *Note: Use template ...*	

When you want to mention a lot of information material, a separate column might be advisable. It's also easier to include links to documents or webpages this way:

Action	Information	Done
Send invitation	Use template ...	

Responsible Parties

When you work on a checklist with a colleague or if the checklist involves assigning tasks to different people, add a column to reflect responsibility:

Action	Responsible
...	

Results

When there is more to an action than the question *if* it has been completed or not, you want to give yourself the space to take notes by adding a suitable column:

Comments

If the outcome of a task can only fall into certain categories, why not structure your checklist accordingly?

Test	Pass	Fail
...		

Time and Effort

If your working through the checklist will later be relevant for a time sheet, remind yourself to make a note of the required data:

Action	Time Spent
...	

Combinations

Most elements of the previous sections can be combined with each other. When you do that, I recommend you choose a structure and stick to it. For example, when you have decided to use a separate column for references to information material, all references should be in that column – rather than having some in the action column and some in the reference column. Updating the checklist will be so much easier.

It's a different matter when the results you want to register on your checklist vary, i.e., if they are not of the same type.

✗ Alice owns a holiday home for rent. She uses a checklist to check the condition of the home before the next guests arrive. When she does the check, she also takes a reading of the electricity meter. She has included a respective action on her checklist. With results filled in, it could like this:

Action	Result
Water boiler	*ok*
Electricity meter reading (kWh)	*37,216*
Bathroom lamp	*ok*

Perhaps she has someone who checks the apartment for her. She wants the checklist to give them more guidance, so they don't just note that the water boiler and the electricity meter are there. She states in the field what the required entry is (e.g., in a lighter colour). The actual result is to be written into the fields over the text, preferably with a coloured pen.

Action	Result	
Water boiler	ok	not ok
Electricity meter reading	kWh	
Bathroom lamp	ok	not ok

Should the person conducting the check have a neglectful handwriting, the form of the checklist might be even more specific:

Action	Result	
Water boiler	ok	not ok
Electricity meter reading (kWh)		
Bathroom lamp	ok	not ok

'This is getting quite sophisticated,' you might object. 'I see myself doing more work on the layout than on the contents. Why can't I just put the checks in a list and add reading for electricity, gas and water at the bottom?'

You can do that, of course, and if it works for you, go ahead. Your checklist will likely have a clearer structure – tasks in the first half, taking readings at the bottom. The disadvantage is that the checklist will assist you less with the order you do things in. If the electricity meter happens to be in the bathroom, you will have to remember by yourself to take the reading while you are checking the room.

*

Feel free to experiment and combine the elements presented in this chapter in any way you find useful. If you have ideas for further structural elements, make a note now.

Having filled our design toolbox, we are now ready to turn to the main thing – content.

Generating Content

This chapter covers getting content, reviewing and checking it. We will discuss how can you make sure a checklist includes the necessary steps to arrive at the required results. These concepts will be explained in the following:

· *Exploration* will show you how to generate and gather content. In an early stage that content may not constitute a task yet, but should be suitable to be transformed into such.

· *Document Review* is a way to derive tasks from existing documents.

· *Simulation* is a technique for a practical review of your checklist. You can always read a checklist and try to find missing steps, but this technique makes wrong or missing steps more visual.

· *Working Backwards* is an approach that focuses on identifying required results and outcomes. Defining the actions to achieve these results will usually take a separate step. You can use the *Simulation* technique for a cross-check afterwards.

Exploration

In a perfect world, you have done before whatever tasks are at hand. And not only would you have done them, but also have taken note of what has been done. A time-tested checklist has formed almost on its own. – That is rarely the case. If you are lucky, there is an old checklist, but it doesn't really match reality anymore.

Another common situation is that a series of tasks has reached a scope you think you can no longer remember without aid. That's why you want to put together a checklist.

If there is nothing else to start from, you need to take whatever you can get hold of. If you have some notes, get them. If there are e-mails that reflect what you did last time, go through them.

Gathering information when there is nothing available in writing is the worst case. Then, you need to gather pieces of information bit by bit. That may mean interviewing a colleague who has done these tasks before and use the answers as a basis.

🛠 In order to illustrate how to explore a new subject, we will use Susan's story that was told on page 5.

Please read it again and try to identify any hints that may indicate a necessary action. You won't come up with a perfect list of tasks in the right order. You may not even know what the required task is. Don't worry about that for now. When you see anything to take care of, make a note.

Before reading on, try for yourself and see what you can come up with.

*

Here are my notes on potential actions based on Susan's story:

Determine staff requirements
Post a job advertisement
Interview applicants
Prepare employment contract
Prepare other paperwork
Welcome new colleague
Hand over welcome package
Hand over access card
Front desk announces the arrival of new hires

> Request computer login details
> Receive computer login details
> Register employee's information in database

Note how we came in just a few minutes from nothing to a dozen items that we can use for building a checklist. There are gaps to fill and preceding or succeeding tasks to add, but we have a basis for going forward.

When you have done some additional work and shuffled the steps around a bit, you will end up with a brand-new checklist of your own. We will come back to this example in the case study on page 48 ff.

Document Review

A *Document Review* works best if we don't know what people did in the past but the outcome is well documented. The idea is to derive the required tasks from the documents that were created in the process.

Relevant documents can be files, e-mails, reports, or invoices if the tasks have been outsourced in the past. In Susan's case, I would recommend reviewing another personnel file.

Go through the documents and consider the following questions for each:

· Who has worked on draft versions?

· Who has prepared the final version?

· Who else has contributed?

· Who has signed it?

· Who has received copies of it (distribution list)?

· Is the document based on a template?

- Are there any formal requirements (e.g., notarization)?
- Does the document specify any actions or other responsibilities?

You can expect to obtain a lot of input for your checklist. Some of it may already describe a specific task. Other notes may require defining tasks and responsibilities.

After you have created a first draft of the checklist, you might wonder if your opus will work in practice. This is where the concept of *Simulation* can help. We will look into that in the next section.

Simulation

When you have made a first draft of a checklist (or if you are confronted with an old checklist you want to use), you need to check if the tasks are complete and in the right order. A good way to find out is to give the checklist to a colleague who has not done these tasks before. Supervising them working through the list will help you to identify many tasks that are not clear, in the wrong place or incomplete.

There is not always a colleague at hand, of course, and the actions of the checklist might stretch over a time period that is too long for a test run. Your alternative is to simulate working through the checklist.

For a *Simulation*, you need your checklist and several slips of paper or index cards. Colleagues are optional – you can do this by yourself, but another pair of eyes may spot additional problems.

Each index card will represent a person (e.g., a hotel guest), a physical object (e.g., a hotel room), or an abstract entity (e.g., a room reservation). On the index cards, we will keep track of the condition and properties of the items they represent. You can move around non-abstract items on the table to reflect their physical location.

Hotel rooms, admittedly, don't have a reputation for getting around much. But let's say the card represents the space of the hotel room. If you find a guest *and* housekeeping in the same room at the same time during the simulation – because the room key was given to the guest before the room had been cleaned – there might be an issue with the checklist.

🛠 Electronic means of communication prevail in these days. We will use the *Simulation* technique to find out if we are still able to send handwritten letters by mail.

Here is the checklist we are going to review:

Checklist: Write Personal Letter

#	Action
1	Take a clean sheet of paper
2	Prepare your favourite pen
3	Write letter
4	Take an envelope that matches the paper
5	Write address on envelope
6	Put stamp in upper right corner of envelope
7	Seal envelope

Let's do a simulation. I will go through the checklist step by step. Feel free to work with me using some index cards:

- **Task 1:** An index card will represent the sheet of paper for the letter. Write 'Sheet of Paper' at the top, so you know what it represents.
- **Task 2:** You can use an index card to represent the pen. You could argue that the pen is just a tool that will be available. If you are comfortable that this is the case, skip the card. If, however, you have a fountain pen worth a week's wages that you fill with special scented ink for the occasion and clean afterwards so it won't dry out – you do need an index card representing the pen.

- **Task 3:** Note on the index card representing the sheet of paper that it now contains the text you want to send.

- **Task 4:** The envelope is a new object. Take another index card and put 'Envelope' on it.

- **Task 5:** Note on the envelope's index card that it shows the address.

- **Task 6:** Note on the envelope's index card that you have attached the stamp. If you are the creative type, you can draw a stamp on the index card – whatever suits you.

- **Task 7:** Note that the envelope is sealed and, thus, ready to be mailed.

And already, we are done with the simulation of the checklist. It works great, right?

☹ No, it does *not* work great! You will probably have spotted the problem already. If not, take a look where the index cards are. They should both be lying on your table. But where is the letter supposed to be when you mail it? Inside the envelope of course!

There is no step on the list to tell you that you have to put the sheet of paper inside the envelope[7].

Doing a simulation by using index cards increases your chances of finding missing or impossible actions.

---

[7] At the risk of overemphasising the point, I repeat that this is exactly why I don't like lists within lists. It seems so logical to divide the checklist of this example into two main actions – writing the letter and preparing the envelope. But when you then look at the sub-lists individually, you risk missing the aspects where they interconnect.

Working Backwards

This a great method when you have no material for a checklist at all, but know what the results should be. The idea is to picture the final result and work backwards from there. The technique works well to generate content for the checklist quickly, but be aware that the tasks won't be in the correct order.

The method works best if you have someone to work with. If you work by yourself, I suggest you write down both the results and intermediate considerations.

🛠 Bob plans to go on holiday and wants to put together a checklist:

Checklist: Planning a Trip

We will interview him with the intention of triggering ideas regarding the preparation of his trip. I will note any topics that come up during the interview under the respective question or answer.

Question: What are your plans for your holiday?
Bob: I want to be on a beach and enjoy the sunshine.

Q: Do you already know where you will be going?
B: Not exactly. I just want to be somewhere warm in a nice hotel.

Determine destination
Book hotel

Q: When exactly are you going?
B: I'm not sure yet. I have to speak with my boss about my substitute while I'm away.

Find substitute
Get approval for annual leave

Q: Let's think about the hotel again. How will you get there?
B: Well, I will go there from the airport.

> Book flight

Q: On foot?
B: No, silly. I will take a taxi. If the hotel has a shuttle, I could use that.

> Get cash in local currency
> Check hotel airport shuttle

B: And before you ask – of course, I will pick up my luggage at the airport first. That reminds me: I may need to buy a new trolley. The old one is a bit small, anyway.

> Check functionality and size of luggage
> Buy new trolley

Q: You are likely travelling overseas, then?

> Valid passport

B: Definitely. Maybe go to a country I have not been before.

> Learn foreign language
> Download language app

B: But I could also go to the Caribbean where they speak English. I could take a course in scuba-diving.

> Look for diving schools
> Get medical check-up

This interview can go on until you feel confident that you have covered all important aspects – e.g., other possible activities during the holiday or what to do about Bob's apartment and mail in the meantime.

Having a basis to work from, you can bring the tasks in a useful order and consider additional points. I am going to re-order the items into three groups, so it becomes easier to review them: formal requirements, bookings and travelling, and activities at destination.

Formal requirements

Find substitute
Get approval for annual leave
Valid passport
Get medical check-up

Reviewing these requirements might remind Bob that a visa or vaccinations could be necessary. Those points can be included in his list.

Bookings and Travelling

Determine destination
Book flight
Book hotel
Check hotel airport shuttle
Check functionality and size of luggage
Buy new trolley

Picturing himself on the plane, Bob might wonder what he will do during the flight. If he wants to take reading material with him, that should be added to the list. But perhaps he prefers to buy something at the airport.

Activities at destination

Get cash in local currency
Look for diving schools
Learn foreign language
Download language app

Apparently, Bob is tempted to do some sightseeing. Should he add 'camera' to his packing list?

Summary

Let's review the four concepts for generating and checking the content of your checklist we have seen in this chapter:

· *Exploration* is for finding material for your checklist. This can include reviewing old or even outdated checklists and interviews. It works best if similar tasks have been done before and you have access to old notes or knowledgeable people.

· *Document Review* works best if you don't have much information about how people reached a target before but the outcome is well documented.

· *Simulation* is helpful when you want to test if your checklist works but you don't have the opportunity or time to apply it to a real case.

· *Working Backwards* is a fallback solution when you have no material at all. You are essentially trying to devise necessary actions or the required documentation by envisaging the intended outcome.

*

This chapter covered techniques for generating and reviewing content. In the previous chapter, we covered elements of layout and structure and how to apply them to a checklist.

You are now ready for the real world and may be confident that you are up to any checklist challenge that you will face in the future.

Then again – if you are not sure yet, you can join me in a case study and see the tools being applied to an example.

Still here? Then let's move on to the next chapter.

Case Study: Susan's Checklist

✘ Susan vividly remembers the awkward situation when she had to tell her new colleagues that their login data was not available and they would have to go without computer access for a couple of days (see page 5). She wants to make sure that this won't happen again and has decided to create a checklist with all important tasks that have to be done before new colleagues arrive on their first day.

As she hasn't used checklists much in the past, she asks you to help her.

Designing the Checklist

You decide to do this by the book[8]. First, we give some thought to the layout. Since you work with Susan, discussing and referring to a specific task is easier when they are numbered (see page 27). You agree to do that.

We have already seen that Susan cannot do all tasks anytime. Rather, there are some things she has to wait for. This is how the problem occurred in the first place. We need a column to put in due dates (see page 28). Also, Susan has every intention of noting the date when she has done something (see page 27).

As it is common that there are several candidates being hired at the same time, Susan will have instances of her checklist (see page 24). Susan wants to add the employee's name, ID number and

---

[8] This book – page 21 ff to be specific.

job title on the checklist. She won't have the employee's ID number at the beginning, but she will be able to add that later.

You argue that it would be convenient to have a column for reference material (see page 33), but Susan insists that she knows *how* to do things and just wants to make sure that she does them in time.

In order to get started quickly, Susan wants the checklist to begin when a job applicant has been selected. She may add earlier activities later (e.g., determine required qualification, job advertisements, interview) and wants to call the checklist 'Recruitment'.

It takes you a few minutes before you can present the general structure of Susan's checklist:

Checklist: Recruitment

Name:
Employee ID:
Job Title:

#	Due	Action	Done

Having done that, we can now turn to the tasks Susan needs to do.

Gathering Content

Susan has already defined when the checklist is meant to start. That gives us a suitable first entry for our checklist:

Advise successful job applicant

If there is a successful candidate, you conclude that there are most like unsuccessful candidates, too.

Inform all unsuccessful job applicants

We can assume that Susan will not inform them until the candidate has accepted the job offer and that she will put on hold other steps as well. Also, she will probably do other things only when the first day of work draws nearer. Let's tentatively fill in the checklist with what we have so far:

#	Due	Action	Done
	★	Advise successful job applicant	
	☐	Do when applicant has accepted job offer[9]	
	↴	Inform all unsuccessful job applicants	
	↴	…	
		Do 2 weeks before new hire starts working	
	↴	…	

We have explored Susan's story in the chapter about 'Exploration' for hints about action items. Here is a list of those that fall within the time frame we want to cover with the checklist (after an applicant has been selected) – feel free to cross them out while we work through them on the following pages:

---

[9] The applicant may indicate his acceptance of the job offer some time after he has been informed that he has been accepted. Accordingly, the applicant accepting the offer is a separate step. We can spare a line if we put the date on which we receive his or her answer in the Done field. Because of that, I will assign a number to this line (see section 'The Final Result' starting on page 54), which I tend not to do for lines that include a condition only.

Prepare employment contract
Prepare other paperwork
Welcome new colleague
Hand over welcome package
Hand over access card
Front desk announces the arrival of new hires
Request computer login details
Receive computer login details
Register employee's information in database

Let's think about the employment contract. First, we need a draft. That draft has to be signed by both parties. Most likely, two copies are required – one for the applicant; the other goes into the personnel file[10]. This is what we get:

Create personnel file[11]
File application documents
Prepare draft of employment contract (2 copies)
Have contracts signed by supervisor
Send employment contracts to applicant
Receive countersigned contract from applicant
File employment contract in personnel file

Putting 'contract' or even 'employment contract' in almost every task might seem tedious, but we cannot be sure that these items will stay in consecutive order. Without context, instructions like 'file it' are hardly helpful, so don't be too parsimonious with words.

---

[10] You noticed that we haven't mentioned 'personnel file' before, right?

[11] We won't have a copy of the employment contract signed by both parties immediately after printing the draft. But since we have chosen one of the applicants, we need a permanent place for the application documents anyway. I have, accordingly, added the line below.

The reference to 'other paperwork' in the next step is quite vague. This may relate to insurance, salary, and taxes. I recommend reviewing another personnel file. That should lead you to all important documents, and required actions can be derived on that basis. The concept of *Simulation* (see page 40) can be used for a crosscheck of the action items.

For the purpose of this case study, I will assume that recording the employee's information in the database will take care of the boring (i.e., standard) stuff – necessary data will be sent automatically to the colleagues in the wage and salary administration, etc.

Regarding taxes, we will likely need further information from the applicant as this is not usually included in the application documents. We get more action items:

> Obtain tax details from successful applicant
> Register employee in database

Additional documentation may be required if the applicant is a foreigner:

> Request proof of work permit[12]

If Susan can skip this action for nationals, this step is conditional. We discussed this case in section 'Conditional Steps' on page 26 ff. Since this is an important *If*, I will use this layout:

---

[12] We will assume that the employment contract includes a clause that renders it void if proof of a work permit is not provided by the applicant. This way, we can prepare the employment contract independently of clarifying his status of residency. Otherwise, the signing of the contact needs to be postponed and the order of the action items on the checklist will have to be changed.

#	Due	Action	Done
	🖑	**If applicant has foreign nationality:** Request proof of work permit	

I am also going to add another entry where the receipt of this information is tracked (page 54 ff – don't look ahead yet).

Let's review what is left open from our original list:

~~Prepare employment contract~~
~~Prepare other paperwork~~
Welcome new colleague
Hand over welcome package
Hand over access card
Front desk announces the arrival of new hires
Request computer login details
Receive computer login details
~~Register employee's name in database~~

The note about welcoming the new hires reminds Susan that the department the applicant is going to work in will be interested in hearing that a job offer was accepted.

Inform department about accepted job offer

They should also select someone who guides the new hire through the first days

Determine main contact at department

Moving on, Susan comes to the conclusion that there are several things she will do only a few days before the candidate starts. The welcome package, for example, contains staff guidelines, and Susan wants to include the latest version. The package can be put together quite quickly, so there is no point in having it laying around for long.

Accordingly, we allow for another series of tasks that are actionable only after a certain date:

#	Due	Action	Done
...			
		Do 3 days weeks before new hire starts working	
	✋	Prepare welcome package	
	✋	Make access card	
	✋	Inform front desk about arrival of new hire	

That leaves us with the dreaded topic of the login details:

> Request computer login details
> Receive computer login details

We also add them to the checklist, so Susan is reminded of them sufficiently early.

The Final Result

By compiling all elements of the previous sections into one list, we get the result on the next page that we can give to Susan.

Checklist: Recruitment

Name:
Employee ID:
Job Title:

#	Due	Action	Done
1	★	Advise successful job applicant	
2	☐	Do when applicant has accepted job offer	
3	↳	Create personnel file	
4	↳	File application documents	
5	↳	Prepare draft of employment contract (2 copies)	
6	↳	Have contracts signed by supervisor	
7	↳	Send employment contracts to applicant	
8	↳	**If applicant has foreign nationality:** Request proof of work permit	
9	↳	Obtain tax details from successful applicant	
10	↳	Receive countersigned contract from applicant	
11	↳	File employment contract in personnel file	
12	↳	Inform department about accepted job offer	
13	↳	Inform all unsuccessful job applicants	
14	↳	Register employee in database	
		Do 2 weeks before new hire starts working	
15	↳	**If applicant has foreign nationality:** Check that proof of work permit has been provided	
16	↳	Determine main contact at department	
17	↳	Request computer login details	
18	↳	Receive computer login details	
19		Do 3 days weeks before new hire starts working	
20	↳	Prepare welcome package	
21	↳	Make access card	
22	↳	Inform front desk about arrival of new hire	

Conclusion

I hope this book will help you unlock the potential that working with checklists holds for your needs and applications. The previous chapters describe the elements that, in my experience, are both fundamental and most versatile. Try those that make sense to you and leave the rest for a later date. In short, be pragmatic – checklists are meant to be used as a tool, not to be an obsession and hopefully not a nuisance.

Obviously, there are endless ways to create a checklist. No book can answer what the best one is in your particular situation. But don't let the desire for the perfect checklist keep your from making one and using it. Here are some tips for getting started:

· Find a place – physical or electronically – where you keep copies of all your checklists. Let your supply of tried and tested samples grow over time. The more checklists you create and use, the easier it will be to create another one.

· Don't collect all checklists you come across. Be selective and limit your collection to checklists you have created yourself and those that include a novel or meaningful element.

· Make a checklist of checklists – checklist you have made, checklists you plan to create, and checklists you consider unnecessary. This will ensure that your checklists are tools you use deliberately rather than randomly.

· I invite you to come back to this book as a work of reference and would like to encourage you to adapt or amend the presented concepts and techniques in any way that's helpful. When you develop other tools on your way to becoming a master checklist maker, add them to your toolbox.

I would very much like to hear from you and about your thoughts on making and using checklists. Feel free to e-mail me at checklists@alexander-nera.com.

Index

actionable 28, 30

ad hoc 12, 22

argument 9

background information 33

benefit 9, 10

business process 14

case study 48

checklist 7, 8, 12, 19, 54

checklist of checklists 56

collection of checklists 56

combinations 34

comment 34

complete 40

complexity 14, 21

condition 26, 29, 52

content 9, 37, 49

cooking pasta 16

date 22, 28

dependency 13

design 21

Document Review 37, 39

documentation 10

due date 28

envelope 42

event 30

Exploration 37

holiday 43

hotel 40

incomplete 40

index card 40

information material 18, 33

instance 24, 28

interview 38, 43

iterative actions 31

layout 21, 48

letter 25, 41

manual 13

meter 35

numbering 17, 27, 29, 50

order 18, 51

packing list 12, 23, 46

pasta 16

personnel file 39, 52

pilots 10

preceding task 30

project office 31, 32

project plan 14

purpose 17

receiver 22

record 28

recurring 13

reference 27

reference material 33

reminder 10

required entry 35

responsibility 33

result 34, 35, 43

sender 22

shopping list 12

Simulation 37, 40

single action 17, 25

standardisation 14

structure 21, 36, 49

sub-list 25, 26, 29, 32, 42

Susan's story 5, 38, 48

template 23

ticking 27, 29

time 34

title 17, 23

to-do list 12

tracking 22

unconditional task 29

update 23, 34

version 22

woodworking 6

Working Backwards 37, 43